GUIDE
TO
GARDENING

CONTENTS

Key to how to grow:

= Grow from seed

= Buy little plants

= Grow from bulbs

You can find tips on how to grow
each plant on page 56 onwards.

See if you can spot the robin on each page.

INTRODUCTION

Imagine a special piece of earth where you can sow, plant and grow anything you like. In this book you'll discover lots of useful tips to help you make a beautiful garden of your very own. You'll also uncover some fascinating stories about the plants and little animals that live in your garden. There are lots of things to make and do on every page too.

Colourful flowers

Juicy raspberries

Sweetly scented herbs

Crunchy carrots

Always wash your hands after gardening and, if you wish, wear gardening gloves. Most plants are perfectly safe. However, a few are poisonous or cause allergies or irritation. Please check with an adult before handling, picking or eating any plants and be careful of sharp objects.

WHAT IS A GARDEN?

A garden can be *very big*.

A garden can be up high!

A garden can be *very small*.

A garden can be *just for you.*

Or somewhere to share: at *school*, in *your town*, with *friends*.

A garden can be *just for you.*

A garden can be far away.

You can make your garden here, there or anywhere.
You don't even need a flower pot!

A garden can be in
the countryside.

A garden can be
in the middle of
a busy city.

Gardens: a place to relax, to play,
to build a den, to make a tree house,
have a picnic, dig for treasures and
grow tasty food and pretty flowers.

WHAT IS A PLANT?

Plants keep us alive. They make the food we eat and the air we breathe. Plants are alive too.
Like us, they breathe, eat and drink, and even know when it's bedtime.

BREATHE, EAT AND DRINK?

Plants have very, very tiny holes in their leaves which let them breathe in and out. Their roots, like straws, take up water and soil minerals too.

SUN CATCHERS

Plants do something truly amazing. They turn sunshine into food.
Leaves are nature's solar panels. Inside them, plants turn sunlight, water and carbon dioxide into a type of sugar (our energy food) and oxygen.

We breathe in oxygen and breathe out carbon dioxide.

Plants take in carbon dioxide and give out oxygen. Perfect!

BEDTIME?
The daisy, or 'day's eye' is
so called because it opens
its flowers in the day
and closes them at night.

Daffodil bulbs go to sleep underground
in the winter and pop up when it
starts to warm up in the spring.

IN YOUR GARDEN
You can help plants along by planting them
in a nice sunny place, watering them
when the soil is dry and feeding the soil.
You can find out all about this in the
mini guide of gardening tips section
from page 56.

THE YEAR IN THE GARDEN: SPRING
March to May

The days get warmer and longer. A busy season in the garden. Time to sow seeds and get growing.

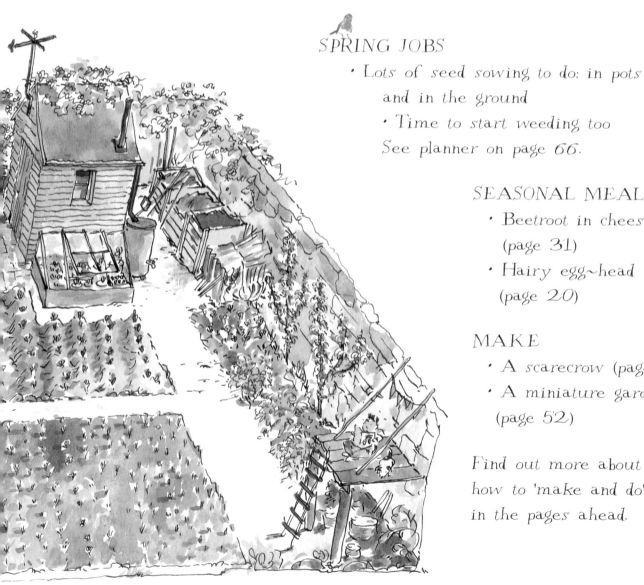

SPRING JOBS
- Lots of seed sowing to do: in pots and in the ground
- Time to start weeding too

See planner on page 66.

SEASONAL MEALS
- Beetroot in cheese sauce (page 31)
- Hairy egg~head (page 20)

MAKE
- A scarecrow (page 45)
- A miniature garden (page 52)

Find out more about how to 'make and do' in the pages ahead.

THE YEAR IN THE GARDEN: SUMMER
June to August

Wonderful long, hot summer days. Everything is growing like crazy. Time to tend your plants, eat summer fruit and vegetables, and of course, picnic and play.

SUMMER JOBS
- Lots of planting out and weeding to do
- Water the soil around your plants when it's dry
- Pick and eat the fruit and vegetables you have grown

See planner on page 66.

SEASONAL MEALS
- Summer picnic (page 54)
- Broccoli trees in mashed potato (page 23)

MAKE
- A den and a guard~it (page 52~53)
- Pot~pourri (page 41)
- Redcurrant cake decorations (page 36)

September to November

The days are drawing in and *sometimes there's* a chill in the air. This is the season of harvesting tasty vegetables and delicious autumn fruits.

AUTUMN JOBS
• Time to tidy up: sweep up the leaves, ask an adult to help you cut back some of the plants.
• Take some plants in pots inside if they don't like the cold. See planner on page 66.

SEASONAL MEALS
• Pumpkin soup (page 28)
• Figgy feasts (page 39)
• Apple pie

MAKE AND DO
• A Halloween pumpkin (page 28)
• A bug hotel (page 47)
• Play apple games (page 38)

Crisp, cold winter days. Plenty to do in the garden to help keep you warm, and winter vegetables to harvest too.

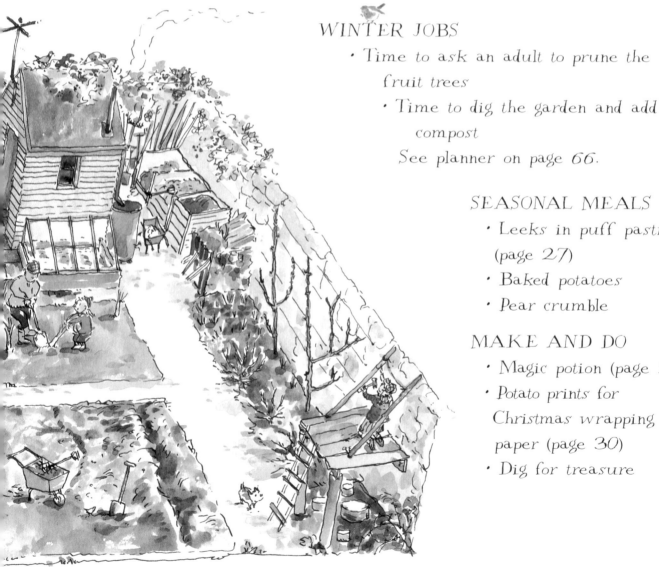

WINTER JOBS
- Time to ask an adult to prune the fruit trees
- Time to dig the garden and add compost

See planner on page 66.

SEASONAL MEALS
- Leeks in puff pastry (page 27)
- Baked potatoes
- Pear crumble

MAKE AND DO
- Magic potion (page 23)
- Potato prints for Christmas wrapping paper (page 30)
- Dig for treasure

HERBS ~ TO GROW IN POTS

Herbs are great plants to start off with in your new garden. They look good, smell nice and are easy to grow in pots. They are used to flavour food. Many help keep you healthy too.

ROSEMARY   *Rosmarinus officinalis*
Victorians put rosemary in the handles of their walking sticks. They used to sniff them thinking they kept diseases away.

THYME   *Thymus vulgaris*
Greeks used to put thyme leaves in their baths. There are many types of thyme. Lemon thyme smells like lemons. Orange~scented thyme has a spicy orange aroma.

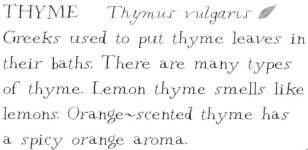

16

BAY   *Laurus nobilis*
Bay is said to help you digest your food.
Pop a leaf in a *stew* to give a lovely flavour,
but take the leaf out before you eat the stew.

MINT   *Mentha*
Mint leaves in hot water make a delicious tea.
No milk needed, but a spoonful of honey
is tasty . . . mmm ~ lovely.

Many herbs come from hot, dry places
so plant them in a warm, sunny spot.

HERBS ~ TO GROW EACH YEAR

DILL *Anethum graveolens*

Dill gets its name from the Anglo~Saxon 'dylle', meaning to 'lull to sleep.'

It was called 'meeting house seed' by the settlers in North America as children chewed it in sermons to stop them from feeling hungry.

Once used as a cold tea for stomach upsets.

It has an aniseed~like taste, great in mashed potatoes.

BASIL *Ocimum basilicum*
Originally from India and the Middle East

How to grow:
Put a stem of basil in
a bottle of water. It will
grow roots in a week
and can be planted in
the garden in spring
and summer.

Tasty with tomatoes and mozzarella cheese and on pizzas.

Keep in a warm place outside
or on a sunny windowsill.
It doesn't like cold frosty weather.

*Purple ruffles basil is
very pretty in salads.*

Make pesto:
Ask an adult to help you blend the basil leaves
with pine nuts, garlic, parmesan cheese and olive
oil. Keeps in a jar in the fridge for a week.
Stir a spoonful into cooked pasta. Simply delicious.

VEGETABLES ~ LEAVES AND SALADS

Sow salad and spinach seeds in rows, pots or even in an old boot filled with soil.

LETTUCE   *Lactuca sativa*

'I had a little lettuce,
I divided it in two.
The leaves I kept myself
and the heart I gave to you'
The middle of a lettuce is called a heart.

ROCKET   *Eruca vesicaria*

Rocket by name, rocket by nature. This fast~growing vegetable is ready to eat four weeks after sowing.

MUSTARD AND CRESS

Brassica hirta and *Lepidium sativum*

Make a hairy egg~head:
When you eat a boiled egg, wash the shell, fill it with seed compost and sow some mustard and cress seeds on top. Paint a face on it. Cut and eat the hairy egg~head's 'hair' after a couple of weeks.

An Italian salad, made of peppery~tasting rocket leaves and slices of juicy orange, is delicious.

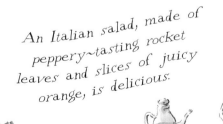

SPICE UP THE SALAD

Colourful nasturtium flowers brighten up vegetable beds, pots and window boxes. Add a couple of petals to salads to spice them up.

NASTURTIUM *Tropaeolum majus*

Their common name comes from the Latin words *nasus* (nose) and *tortus* (twisted). Does its peppery taste make your nose wrinkle up?

Cut and come again mixed salad

SOW	GROW	CUT	COME AGAIN

SOW	GROW	CUT	COME AGAIN
Sow seeds in rows in spring and summer.	Wait for a few weeks.	Ask an adult to cut the leaves for your salad.	After their haircut the plants will grow again.

VEGETABLES ~ THE CABBAGE PATCH

Cabbages, Brussels sprouts, broccoli, cauliflowers, kale, turnips, swedes and radishes are all related. Take a sniff. They all have a similar cabbagy smell and little round seeds too.

KALE *Brassica oleracea*
One of the elders of the cabbage family. Lovely cooked in milk.

RADISH *Raphanus sativus*
Easy and fast growing (six weeks from sowing to eating). Eat them raw: crunchy, peppery and tasty.

In Oaxaca city, Mexico, they celebrate the Noche de Rabânos ~ 'Night of the Radishes' ~ on 23rd December. They carve giant radishes into beautiful shapes and process through the streets.

CAULIFLOWER
Brassica oleracea
Comes in red and purple as well as white.
'The cauliflower is nothing but a cabbage
with a college education' ~ Mark Twain

RED CABBAGE
Brassica oleracea

Make magic potion:
Ask an adult to cut up and boil a red cabbage.
Eat it up and keep the purple water.
Add lemon juice then bicarbonate
of soda to the cabbage water.
What colour does it go?

WARNING ~ DO NOT DRINK

BROCCOLI *Brassica oleracea*
In Italian, broccoli means 'little shoots'.
Ask an adult to steam it gently and
put on to a pile of mashed potato to
make a hill with trees on. It's a great
way of getting your little brother or
sister to eat up their greens ~
which are really good for you.

VEGETABLES ~ PEAS AND BEANS

RUNNER BEAN *Phaseolus coccineus*
Sow May and June. Harvest August
to October.
Jack planted his bean and grew
a very big beanstalk. How tall will
yours grow?

TURNING AIR INTO FOOD
Peas and beans have friendly
bacteria living in knobbles on
their roots which turn air into
plant fertilizer. These plants
are really good for the garden.

FRENCH BEANS *Phaseolus vulgaris*
French beans are from America, not France.
They were brought to Europe by the Spanish
conquistadors. Delicious steamed with chopped
tomatoes on.

PEAS *Pisum sativum*
Many *sorts*: green, purple, tall, petit pois
(little peas), mange~tout (eat pods
and all).

Peas and beans clamber and climb so give them sticks to grow up.

Grow beansprouts *Vigna radiata*
Put mung beans in a jam jar with
muslin on top.
Add water for three hours, then strain.
Rinse with clean water every day.
Eat the beansprouts when they are big
enough ~ yummy in salads and stir~fries.

You could have a den inside!

WARNING
Some relations of peas and beans, such as sweet peas and laburnum
seeds, are very poisonous. Never eat them. Just enjoy looking at their
beautiful flowers.

VEGETABLES ~ THE ONION FAMILY

ONION   *Allium cepa* 🧅

Fried onions taste good with hot dogs on bonfire night. Ask an adult to slice and cook them. Give the adult a handkerchief ~ chopping onions makes your eyes water!

Plant baby onion 'sets' in spring for a bumper crop in autumn.

GARLIC   *Allium sativum* 🧄

Magical plant: in stories garlic is said to keep off vampires.

Growing plant: plant one piece (a clove of garlic) in spring and it will grow into a whole bulb by late summer.

Healthy plant: in ancient times Egyptians gave garlic to the slaves who built the pyramids to keep them fit and healthy.

LEEK   *Allium porrum*

The national symbol of Wales (along with the daffodil).
The Roman emperor Nero was said to have liked his leek soup.

Sow seeds in March/April.
When large enough to handle (May~June time)
transplant into holes made with a dibber in
freshly dug ground.

There are world leek championships
with prizes of over £1000. Before
the show, leek champions have
been known to give their
leeks a bubble bath and
brush their roots!

CHIVES

Allium schoenoprasum
Eat the pretty purple
flowers and the leaves
in salads.

Make a tasty supper:
Help an adult to wrap leeks
in puff pastry then enjoy them
baked with cheese sauce.

VEGETABLES ~ PUMPKINS, FRIENDS AND RELATIONS

PUMPKIN   *Cucurbita maxima*

Cinderella's fairy godmother turned a pumpkin and white mice into a magical coach with white horses to take her to the ball.

Pumpkin comes from a Greek word, 'pepon'. It means 'cooked by the sun'.

Make a Halloween pumpkin:

Ask an adult to help you scoop out the seeds and some of the flesh of a pumpkin, carve a picture in the side, put a candle inside to make a beautiful lantern. The scooped~out pumpkin flesh makes a delicious soup.

SQUASH *Cucurbita maxima*

Originated in America and now popular
in many parts of the world. Sweet and
tasty when baked. They come in all
shapes and sizes and colours:

COURGETTE AND MARROW

Cucurbita pepo

Courgettes are baby marrows.

Fun grown big

Ask an adult to help you carve your initials
or a face into the skin of a growing courgette
~ and over the weeks watch it grow and grow.

Tasty eaten small
Grill with cheese on top.

VEGETABLES ~ GROWING UNDERGROUND

POTATOES *Solanum tuberosum*

One of the most important food crops in the world, along with wheat, rice and maize. Eat potatoes boiled, fried, chipped or mashed.

Make potato prints:

Ask an adult to help you cut a potato in half and cut a pattern into it. Then dip into paint, and off you go. If you use cloth paint, you could design your own T~shirt.

Grow your own:

| Early spring | Late spring | Early summer | Late summer |

Put 'seed' potatoes (baby potatoes) in a warm, sunny room for about four weeks until shoots grow.

Plant potatoes outside in a trench containing compost. Cover with soil.

Every two weeks put earth over them as they grow.

Dig up delicious potatoes.

WARNING ~ Green potato tubers are poisonous so keep them in a dark place to stop them turning green.

CARROT   *Daucus carota*

- Crunchy and juicy raw. Sweet and soft cooked
- Make delicious cakes and lip~smacking soups
- Carrots come in white or purple as well as orange
- Once carrot leaves were used to decorate hats

Tip: Pesky carrot fly grubs eat the roots. Planting onions next to them helps keep the carrot fly away.

BEETROOT   *Beta vulgaris*

- Bake like potatoes
- Boil and serve with cheese sauce, which turns pink!
- Borsch: beetroot soup with added soured cream

Tips:
- *Water carrots and beetroot if the soil gets very dry.*
- *Small garden? Grow them in tubs or sacks of soil.*

31

VEGETABLES ~ A TASTE OF SUMMER

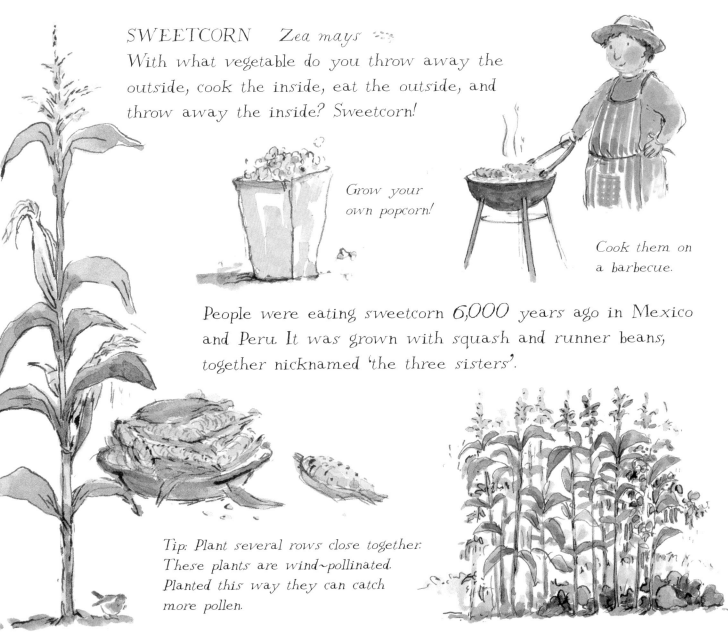

SWEETCORN   *Zea mays*
With what vegetable do you throw away the outside, cook the inside, eat the outside, and throw away the inside? Sweetcorn!

Grow your own popcorn!

Cook them on a barbecue.

People were eating sweetcorn 6,000 years ago in Mexico and Peru. It was grown with squash and runner beans, together nicknamed 'the three sisters'.

Tip: Plant several rows close together. These plants are wind~pollinated. Planted this way they can catch more pollen.

TOMATOES *Solanum lycopersicum*

European explorers brought back tomatoes from Mexico in the 1500s. At first people only grew them to look at because they thought they were poisonous. Today we eat them in salads, soups and on pasta and pizza.

Make your own tomato sauce:

Ask an adult to chop garlic and celery and fry in olive oil. Add mushed~up tomatoes. Cook for 10 minutes. Add pinches of salt, pepper, brown sugar and a dash of vinegar. Ask an adult to whiz it up in a food processor.

Why did the tomato go red?
Because it saw the salad dressing.

How to grow tomatoes:

Pinch out the little side shoots as they grow.

Tap the plants gently when in flower as this helps the fruits to grow.

Feed with tomato food following the instructions on the label. Pick tomatoes when ripe.

SOFT FRUIT Tasty and full of vitamins to keep you healthy.

STRAWBERRIES *Fragaria ananassa*

What is the only fruit with the seeds on the outside?
A strawberry.

WINTER: Plant in compost~rich soil in a big pot or in the garden. Sprinkle fresh compost around the plant every year.

SPRING: Watch the flowers appear.

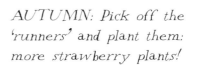

SUMMER: Pick delicious strawberries.

AUTUMN: Pick off the 'runners' and plant them: more strawberry plants!

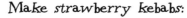

Make strawberry kebabs:
Thread strawberries on to a stick and put them in the freezer for a delicious lolly on a hot day.

RASPBERRIES   *Rubus idaeus*

Magic wands: What stick can turn garden compost into delicious red fruit?
A raspberry cane!

WINTER: Plant autumn raspberry canes in compost~rich soil.

SPRING AND SUMMER: Watch them grow.

AUTUMN: Pick delicious raspberries.

WINTER: In February ask an adult to cut the canes down to just above the ground. Add garden compost.

Make raspberry fool:

Ingredients:
2 cups of raspberries, mashed with ¼ cup of sugar.
1 cup of double cream, whipped with ¼ cup of sugar.
Mix together, pop in fridge for a couple of hours, then eat.

35

BUSH FRUIT

GOOSEBERRY   *Ribes uva~crispa*

Why are they called gooseberries? Because:

- Gooseberry sauce was eaten with roast goose?
- Their thorny branches look like goose feet?

You decide and see if you can think of some other ideas too.

REDCURRANTS   *Ribes rubrum*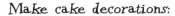

Make cake decorations:
Dip washed tangy berries in lightly whisked egg white and roll them in sugar to make them sweet and frosty~looking.

Chop chop

Ask an adult to help you prune your fruit bushes in the winter. This will help them make more fruit.

- Cut out some of the central branches to stop them getting crowded.
- Cut back the tips of some outer branches by about a third.

BLACKCURRANTS *Ribes nigrum*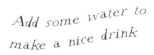

During the Second World War it was difficult to get hold of oranges. People were encouraged to grow blackcurrants. Blackcurrant syrup was given free to children under two years old to boost their vitamin C.

Make blackcurrant syrup:
2 cups of blackcurrants
½ cup sugar
1 cup of water
Juice of a lemon
Ask an adult to cook it all up in a saucepan. Squash it, cool it, strain it, bottle it and put in the fridge.

Add some water to make a nice drink

Use as a sauce on ice cream

Chop chop
Every year ask an adult to cut a third of the old wood of your blackcurrant bush down to the ground.

TREE FRUIT

APPLE *Malus domestica*
Some apple trees in orchards
are old, big and tall.
Others in small gardens are
trained against a wall.
Miniature trees can be grown
in pots too.
So whatever the size of your
garden there's a tree to suit you.

*'An apple a day keeps
the doctor away.'
Apples contain healthy
nutrients. They may be
good for you, but brush
your teeth after eating
them as they contain
lots of natural sugar.*

Make a party game:
*Ask an adult to thread some apples on to string and hang them
from a branch. Try eating them ~ without using your hands!*

PLUM *Prunus domestica*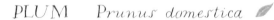

Plum and cherry blossoms celebrate the arrival
of spring; they are the first trees in the
orchard to flower. This keeps the bees happy.
They feed on the nectar and pollinate the flowers. The bit
in the middle of the flower can then grow into a fruit.

FIG TREE *Ficus carica*

Greek athletes ate lots of figs,
they thought it would make them run faster.

*Tip: grow your fig tree in a pot, and when the leaves fall
off in autumn pop it in a dark frost~free shed until spring.*

Make a figgy feast:

*For a real treat ask an adult to cut a fig in half,
brush with olive oil and honey and bake until it
bubbles. Cool a little and serve with ice cream. Yum!*

39

FUN WITH FLOWERS

SUMMER BLOOMS: SUNFLOWERS   *Helianthus annuus*

Sow in spring. See who can grow the tallest.
In 2012 a man in Germany grew a
sunflower 8.23m (27ft) tall!

AUTUMN BLOOMS: OBEDIENT PLANT
Physostegia virginiana
Bend the individual flowers of this
well~behaved plant and they stay
where they are put.

SPRING BLOOMS:

BLEEDING HEART,
LADY IN THE BATHTUB
Lamprocapnos spectabilis

Look closely. Can you spot
the lady in the bathtub?

DAFFODILS   *Narcissus*
Many bulbs grow and flower before the trees
come into leaf and shade the ground.

40

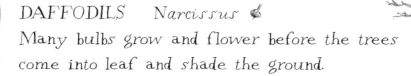

Make your own pot~pourri

Cut and dry these plants to scent a room.

Rose petals and buds   Lavender flowers

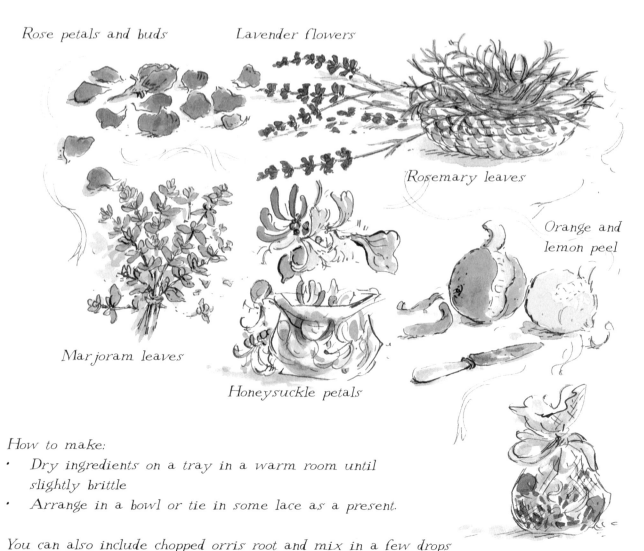

Rosemary leaves

Orange and
lemon peel

Marjoram leaves

Honeysuckle petals

How to make:
- Dry ingredients on a tray in a warm room until slightly brittle
- Arrange in a bowl or tie in some lace as a present.

You can also include chopped orris root and mix in a few drops of rose or lavender fragrant oils, both can be bought and help keep it smelling nice for longer.

WHO ARE YOU CALLING A WEED?

A weed is just a plant growing in the wrong place.
Many weeds are just very successful wild plants.

DANDELION *Taraxacum officinale*

Dandelions produce fluffy, parachute~shaped seeds
that the wind can carry for miles.

**Make a tick~tock
dandelion clock:**
How many puffs does it take
to blow all the seeds away?
One o'clock? Two o'clock?

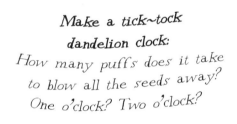

DOCK

Rumex obtusifolius
A tiny piece of root,
even when dried out
for months, can grow
into a whole new plant.

CHICKWEED *Stellaria media*

One plant can make about 15,000
million more new plants a year.
Each plant has about 2,500 seeds.
Each seed can grow into
a new plant in seven weeks.

Gardeners like to get rid of weeds as they compete with the other plants for water, light and food.

TUG
Dig them out, roots and all, before they flower. 'One year's seeding, seven years weeding.'

HOE, HOE, HOE
On dry days hoe out the weeds between rows of vegetables.

MULCH
Cover the ground around trees and bushes with straw or wood chips. No light ~ no weeds.

FRIEND . . . OR FOE?

Your garden is your very own backyard safari park. Look carefully and see who you can find.

These 'predators' eat the pests that eat your plants.

LADYBIRD AND LARVAE
Ladybirds and their babies (larvae) eat aphids.

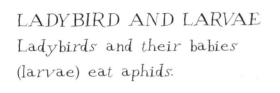

HOVERFLY AND LARVAE
Hoverfly larvae eat aphids. Adult hoverflies hover and sip nectar. Attract them with yellow~centred flowers.

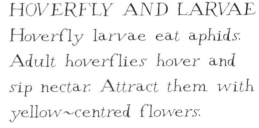

Toads and hedgehogs eat slugs.

Some types of garden birds eat caterpillars.

These pests may eat or harm your plants.

APHIDS
These little
insects suck
plant sap and
damage plants.

CABBAGE WHITE BUTTERFLY
This butterfly's caterpillars
eat cabbage.

SLUGS AND SNAILS . . .
. . . chomp your plants. Catch them
under half~grapefruit skins.

Make a scarecrow:
Help keep birds from scratching up seedlings
in the vegetable patch.

1. *Make a frame with sticks and string*
2. *Make a head from a leg cut off some old tights*
   stuffed with straw or leaves
3. *Add some old clothes stuffed with straw*
   or leaves

45

GO WILD IN THE GARDEN

More houses and roads mean fewer wild places for wildlife. You can help by making a wildlife garden to grow food for wildife.

SUNFLOWERS
Helianthus annuus.
Seeds for birds.

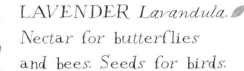

LAVENDER *Lavandula.*
Nectar for butterflies
and bees. Seeds for birds.

HONEYSUCKLE
Lonicera. Nectar for
butterflies and moths.
Berries for birds.

THYME *Thymus*
Nectar for bees.
Home for little bugs.

ICE PLANT *Sedum*
spectabile Autumn
nectar for butterflies,
bees and hoverflies.

All the trees, bushes, grasses and flowers in your garden provide homes for wildlife. You could also . . .

Make a bug hotel:

Use natural and recycled materials to give lots of small spaces in different shapes and sizes, some dry and some damp.

The guest list of garden friends:
- Ladybirds and lacewings sleeping over winter (hibernating)
- Leaf~cutter bees looking for a place to nest
- Ground beetles looking for a dark wooden room
- Spiders needing a place to spin
- Woodlice wanting a damp room
- Woodlice~crunching spiders wanting a room close by

THE BIRDS IN THE GARDEN

See who you can spot in your garden.

House sparrow

Blackbird

Great tit

Starling

Wood pigeon

Chaffinch

Collared dove

Blue tit

Robin

Make a checklist:
Keep a list of the birds you see.
Some people do this every year.
It provides a record of which
birds are becoming more common
and which rarer.

THE BEES

Plants don't move much so they use pollinators, such as bees, to carry pollen from one flower to another. This fertilizes the flower so it can make seeds and fruits.

Some flowers make sugary nectar to thank the bees for their help. The bees make it into honey. So ～ bees help bring us honey and apples.

MAKING A BEE LINE

Some flowers have special markings which direct the bee to its centre, where the pollen is. Bees see differently to us.

We see evening primroses like this:

Bees see them like this:

THE BUTTERFLIES

See if you can *spot* any of *these butterflies in your garden.*

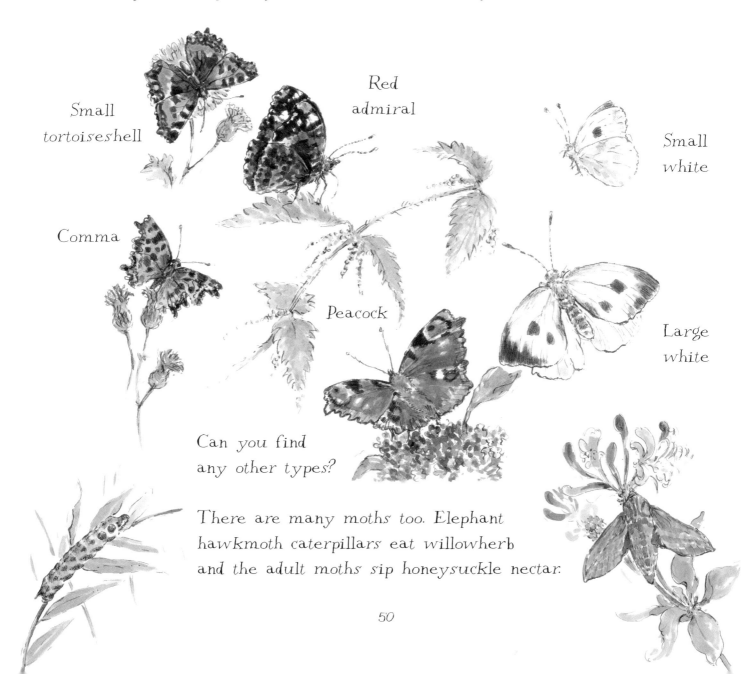

Small
tortoiseshell

Red
admiral

Small
white

Comma

Peacock

Large
white

Can you find
any other types?

There are many *moths* too. Elephant
hawkmoth caterpillars eat *willowherb*
and the adult moths sip honeysuckle nectar.

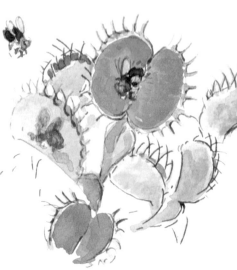

PLANTS THAT MOVE
Some plants can move . . . a bit.

THE VENUS FLY~TRAP
Dionaea muscipula
This plant grows in soil that doesn't contain much plant food. It needs something else to eat. Meat!

This plant can also count! The fly climbs inside. It touches one hair on its trap, nothing happens. If it touches a second hair within 20 seconds ~ the trap closes. SNAP.

SENSITIVE PLANT *Mimosa pudica*
Touch the leaves and they collapse. Why? Maybe to put off animals that might otherwise eat them. After about half a hour the plant recovers.

Both the plants above can be grown in a pot on a sunny windowsill. Be gentle. Poking them too much will finish them off

MODELS AND GAMES

Make a miniature garden:
Plan *your* perfect garden in a tray
or box before making the real thing.
Tips:

- Little twigs make great
  tiny trees
- Little flowers make pretty
  flower bushes
- Green grass mowings can
  make a little lawn

Make a guard~it:
Mix *soil* and *water* into a *sticky* ball.
Add *twigs*, feathers and flowers to make
a face. At the Eden Project in Cornwall
we hang these magical creatures outside
our dens to bring good luck.

Make a den:

Tips:

- Useful den kit includes: canes, sticks, string, old sheets, clothes pegs, big cardboard boxes
- Avoid heavy or sharp things. Be careful not to poke yourself in the eye when working with sticks or canes
- Stick tripods make dens stronger
- Push live willow stems into the ground ~ they will grow roots and make a living den.

Rules:

- Respect nature. Don't damage living plants when making your den
- Respect the garden. Tidy up afterwards

Shhh!
If you sit quietly inside your den you can watch the garden wildlife.

A CELEBRATORY SUMMER PICNIC

Party time. Time to relax and play with friends on a warm, sunny day . . . and, of course, have a delicious picnic.
Can you spot the plants that have been grown in the garden?

YOUR MINI GUIDE OF GARDENING TIPS

GET STARTED

Make a list of what you want to grow. Don't try everything at once ~ there is always next year. Draw a plan of what you want to plant where. Watch your plot: see where it is sunny, shady, dry, wet... Some plants do better in certain places.

CHOOSE THE RIGHT TOOL FOR THE JOB

Spade: for digging and moving soil

Hoe: for hoeing out weeds

Fork: for digging looser soil and removing weeds

Rake: for levelling soil and making it crumbly

Trowel: for digging small holes

MAKE IT EASIER . . . TOGETHER
There is always something new to learn. Ask parents, grandparents, and gardeners in your neighbourhood whom you know well.
Do you have a school garden? If not, see if you and your friends can help your teachers start one.

Ask an adult to find out if there is a community garden in your area, and garden together.

THE ANSWER LIES IN THE SOIL

Many creatures
call *soil* home too.

Worms

Fungi

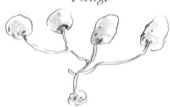

Woodlice

Bacteria

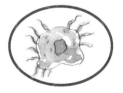

These bacteria are
tiny, 7 billion would fit
on the head of a pin.

Roots anchor the plant
in the ground and take
up plant food (minerals)
and *water*. The *soil*
is their home and
their larder.

The best gardening tip of all: look after the soil and it will look after your plants and make them big and strong.

Soil contains sand, silt, clay, organic matter, soil creatures and passages containing air, water and food. Soil is like a store cupboard in a kitchen.

Soil creatures, the hidden helpers, eat dead plant matter, turn it into plant food and help dig the soil.

LOOKING AFTER YOUR SOIL

Good gardeners look after their soil really, really well.

FOOD
They feed the soil with fertilizer
and compost.

WATER
They water it when
it is really dry.

DIG
They dig it when it gets
hard, especially in the
autumn and winter, to let
the frost get into it and
make it spongy again.

PROTECT

They cover it with plants and compost to stop the rain washing out the plant food. They try not to walk on it ~ they don't want to squash the little spaces and passages inside it.

Make garden compost:

Help grown~ups look after their soil.
Ask them to collect organic waste: weeds, grass cuttings, uncooked vegetable peelings, even ripped~up black~and~white newspapers. Mix it in a compost bin. In a few months it will have turned into brown crumbly garden compost. Dig it into the garden and it will make the soil just right.

GROW FROM SEED

When to sow? Check the planner on page 66.
Some seeds are sown in pots indoors in a sunny spot. Others can go straight outside.

- Read the packet. Follow any special instructions.

- Make a 'seed bed'. Dig then rake the soil to give a level, crumbly surface.

- Mark out a row. Make a shallow groove along it with a stick.

- Sprinkle seeds along the groove.

- Cover with a thin layer of soil.

- Care for seedlings. Water when dry. If lots come up, use a lollipop stick as a baby spade to dig up and replant some to give them all more room.

GROW FROM LITTLE PLANTS

Not all plants in the garden need to be grown from seed.

BABY PLANTS
Many plants, called perennials, live for several years. These can be bought as baby plants in pots. As they grow, plant them in potting compost in bigger pots, keep them in a warm, sunny spot, water the soil when it starts to dry out and watch them grow bigger and bigger.

HERBS
Some, such as thyme, can be planted in the garden. (see page 16).

Mint is best kept in a pot ~ otherwise the roots will grow and grow and grow across the garden. (see page 17).

POTATOES
These are grown from baby potatoes ~ called seed potatoes. See how to grow them on page 30.

GROW FROM BULBS

BULBS

Daffodil bulbs are planted underground in the autumn. They produce beautiful flowers in the spring.

> **WARNING**
> **NEVER EAT DAFFODIL BULBS**
> **~ THEY ARE POISONOUS.**

Onion sets and cloves of garlic are also types of bulb. These are planted in the garden in spring with the pointy end just poking up above the surface of the soil. They grow all summer long and can be harvested in the autumn. See page 26.

MAKE MORE OF WHAT YOU HAVE

STRAWBERRY RUNNERS
Ask an adult to cut these off
and plant in rows or pots.

CUTTINGS
Some plants grow from cuttings ~ pieces
of stem. Pruned stems of blackcurrant,
gooseberry or redcurrant can be
pushed into the ground to root.
Make sure they are the right
way up. They take about
a year to root.

Tip: Willow roots grow
easily. To help other
cuttings grow roots,
soak willow stems in
water and water the
cuttings with that.

PLANNER

	Spring			Summer		
	March	April	May	June	July	August
Potato						
Tomato						
Pea						
French and runner bean						
Kale						
Red cabbage						
Green broccoli						
Purple~sprouting broccoli						
Radish						
Spinach						
Salads						
Rocket						
Courgette						
Squash						
Pumpkin						
Sweetcorn						
Garlic, onion						
Leek						
Carrot, beetroot						
Herb from seed						
Flowers from seed						
Beansprouts, mustard and cress						

When to plant the plants you buy:
- Plant fruit bushes and trees 🌿 in winter (on a day when it's not too frosty).
- Plant the *softer herbaceous plants* 🌿 in autumn or spring ~ e.g. rosemary, mint, bleeding heart and the obedient plant.

This is your guide to when to sow, plant and harvest. Timings depend on where you live: plants take longer to grow when it's colder.

	Autumn			Winter		
	September	October	November	December	January	February
Potato	▓					
Tomato	▓	▓				▓▓
Pea	▓	▓				
French and runner bean	▓	▓				
Kale	▓	▓	▓	▓	▓	
Red cabbage	▓	▓	▓	▓		
Green broccoli	▓	▓				
Purple-sprouting broccoli			▓	▓		
Radish	▓	▓	▓			
Spinach	▓	▓	▓	▓	▓	
Salads	▓	▓	▓	▓	▓	
Rocket	▓	▓	▓	▓	▓	
Courgette	▓					
Squash	▓					
Pumpkin	▓	▓	▓			
Sweetcorn	▓					
Garlic, onion						
Leek		▓	▓	▓	▓	▓
Carrot, beetroot	▓	▓				
Herb from seed	▓					
Flowers from seed	▓					
Beansprouts, mustard and cress	▓	▓	▓	▓	▓	▓

There are so many things you can grow in the garden. Here are three ideas of easy things to get you started:
- Easy to grow: rocket, salad and radish
- Good to grow in a pot: chives, tomatoes and basil
- Tasty eaten raw: radish, salad and peas

INDEX

TICK~LIST OF PLANTS GROWN

Tick off the plant when you've grown it

- ☐ Apple
- ☐ Basil
- ☐ Bay
- ☐ Beansprouts
- ☐ Beetroot
- ☐ Blackcurrants
- ☐ Bleeding heart
- ☐ Broccoli
- ☐ Carrot
- ☐ Cauliflower
- ☐ Chives
- ☐ Courgette and marrow
- ☐ Daffodil
- ☐ Dill
- ☐ Fig
- ☐ French beans
- ☐ Garlic
- ☐ Gooseberry
- ☐ Honeysuckle
- ☐ Ice plant
- ☐ Kale
- ☐ Lavender
- ☐ Leek

- ☐ Lettuce
- ☐ Mint
- ☐ Nasturtium
- ☐ Obedient plant
- ☐ Onion
- ☐ Peas
- ☐ Plum
- ☐ Potatoes
- ☐ Pumpkin
- ☐ Radish
- ☐ Raspberries
- ☐ Red cabbage
- ☐ Redcurrant
- ☐ Rocket
- ☐ Rosemary
- ☐ Runner beans
- ☐ Salad
- ☐ Squash
- ☐ Strawberries
- ☐ Sunflowers
- ☐ Sweetcorn
- ☐ Thyme
- ☐ Tomatoes

MY GARDENING SCRAPBOOK

These are your very own pages for keeping a record of everything you see and do in your garden during the year.

Use them as a diary, to list your garden ideas, draw or paint plants you'd like to grow. You could even use the pages to press your favourite leaves or flowers or stick in photos of things you have made for the garden.

Don't forget to:
· Make a note of the wildlife you see in your garden
· Date all your entries

This could be a very useful document one day.

The headings on the following pages are suggestions only ~ use the space as you wish and let your imagination run wild.

Happy gardening!

THE GARDEN IN SUMMER

THE GARDEN IN AUTUMN

To my father, John, who introduced me to the magic of gardening
when I was two and who has been a lifelong inspiration.
Thank you. xxx ~ J.E

To Susan, my green fingered mother in law. With love x E.T.

A LITTLE GUIDE TO GARDENING
AN EDEN PROJECT BOOK 978 0 957 49072 7
Published in Great Britain by Eden Project Books,
an imprint of Random House Children's Publishers UK
A Penguin Random House Company

Penguin
Random House
UK

This edition published 2015
1 3 5 7 9 10 8 6 4 2
Text copyright © Jo Elworthy, 2015. Illustrations copyright © Eleanor Taylor, 2015. The right of Jo Elworthy and Eleanor Taylor to
be identified as the author and illustrator of this work has been asserted in accordance with the Copyright, Designs and Patents Act 1988.
All rights reserved.
Set in TW WILD FLOWERS; devised by Charlotte Voake
RANDOM HOUSE CHILDREN'S PUBLISHERS UK, 61-63 Uxbridge Road, London W5 5SA
www.randomhousechildrens.co.uk www.edenproject.com www.randomhouse.co.uk
Addresses for companies within The Random House Group Limited can be found at: www.randomhouse.co.uk/offices.htm
THE RANDOM HOUSE GROUP Limited Reg. No. 954009
A CIP catalogue record for this book is available from the British Library.

Printed in China

The Eden Project, an educational charity in Cornwall, built a
global garden in a massive crater that once used to be a china
clay pit. Eden creates gardens, exhibitions, events and projects
that help connect us with each other and the living world.
www.edenproject.com